CW01651490

your first book of

herb gardening

In the same series
Your First Book of Ballet
Your First Book of Riding

Angus & Robertson Publishers
London . Sydney . Melbourne . Singapore . Manila

This book is copyright. Apart from any fair dealing for the purposes of private study, research, criticism or review, as permitted under the Copyright Act, no part may be reproduced by any process without written permission. Inquiries should be addressed to the publishers.

First published by Angus & Robertson Publishers, Australia, 1980

© Elizabeth Hemphill 1980

National Library of Australia
Cataloguing-in-publication data.

Hemphill, Elizabeth.
Your first book of herb gardening.

Index
For children
ISBN 0 207 14353 6

I. Herb gardening — Juvenile literature.
II. Title.

635.7

Design Neil Carlyle
Photography Gary Isaacs, John Hemphill

Printed in Hong Kong

ELIZABETH HEMPHILL
illustrated by DAVID MITCHELHILL

your first book of herb gardening

ANGUS & ROBERTSON PUBLISHERS

Herbs in the garden

1

Hundreds of years ago, herbs and vegetables were the main part of people's gardens. They were picked daily to be used not only in cooking, but also to make medicines to treat the family's coughs and colds, stomach aches, toothaches, and other ailments. In those days there were no chemist shops to go to, but usually people managed very well just using their herbal remedies. We can imagine how charming and sweet-smelling these gardens were.

Maybe your parents already have a large garden and there is no room for you to have your own section. Don't worry, herbs can be planted in a flower or vegetable bed very successfully. But you must know how tall a plant will grow (see all the details you'll need to know about the most common herbs in the next chapter) before you start adding to a garden, or you might find that the lavender you have planted has grown and covered up some tiny violets or other special things! Also be sure that the position you have chosen will give your herb the right amount of sunshine — for example, peppermint geraniums and mint like to grow in moist, shady spots, while most other herbs prefer lots of sunshine.

There are many low-growing herbs such as creeping thymes and prostrate rosemary, as well as garden thyme, savory and chervil, which can be planted along the front edge of a garden bed, giving a pretty and fragrant border. Larger herbs that can be planted amongst flowers are lavender, rosemary, scented geraniums, dill and wormwood. When they are kept trimmed, both lavender and rosemary can be used to make a thick wall or hedge which can attractively line a path, driveway or shrubbery.

See Chapter 4 for ideas for other convenient places to grow your herbs. You can grow them in a rockery, in a vegetable garden (and actually keep pests away if you choose the right herbs), and even in pots if you live in a flat or are just short of space. But first you will need to know the characteristics of the most common herbs so you can choose which ones you would like to plant.

Herbs are either "annual" or "perennial". Annuals

are plants which die off in the winter time and need to be replanted the following spring. Some herbs such as parsley will "self-sow" easily, which means that the seeds that drop from the flowers will lie in the ground and begin to grow up around the parent plant without your having to do any replanting. Perennials are plants which usually last for several years, although some such as thyme, marjoram and oregano tend to become very woody after a few years and need replacing.

All plants belong to certain "families" — groups which share something in common. Most herbs are members of the following groups:

Labiatae:
All plants in this family have lipped flowers like snapdragons.

basil	marjoram	sage
balm	oregano	savory
bergamot	mint	thyme
lavender	rosemary	

Umbelliferae:
Members of this family have umbrella-shaped flowers.

angelica	dill
anise	fennel
carraway	parsley
chervil	

Liliaceae:
All plants in this the lily family have bulb roots.

chives
onion
garlic

Cruciferae:
The flowers in this family are shaped like a cross.

cress
horseradish

There are other herbs which do not belong to these main groups, just as there are plants that are not herbs belonging to the groups mentioned above.

The next chapter is designed to help you choose which herbs will be suitable for your particular garden or need. To make a quick assessment of each one easy for you, symbols have been used to show their special needs and uses:

 needs full sunshine

 needs full sunshine, sheltered from wind

 needs partial sunshine

 grows from seeds

 grows from cuttings

 used in slow cooking, for example, stews

 used in quick cooking, for example, omelettes

 used in oven cooking, for example, roasts and stuffings

 used in salads

 used to make a tea

 used for its perfume

The most common herbs

2

BASIL

This delightful herb, so delicious with tomato salads, can only be grown in the summer which is luckily when tomatoes are plentiful! There are three kinds of basil: bush basil, a compact plant growing to 30 cm tall; sweet basil, a larger-leaved type which grows to 75 cm; and a purple-leaved basil, which adds colour to the garden but has a less pleasant flavour than the others.

Basil was first known in India as a sacred religious herb, but is famous today mainly for its use in Italian cooking. In one part of Romania, in eastern Europe, it is believed that a boy will love for ever the girl from whose hand he accepts a sprig of basil — maybe this is because it is such a delicious herb and good for settling an upset stomach!

All types of basil grow easily from seed, but you must be sure that the spring warmth has really arrived and that all chance of frost is past. If started in a seed tray, sweet basil plants should be put out into a sunny, sheltered position when they are 30 cm tall, with a distance of 30 cm between them. Bush basil, being smaller, only needs a space of 15 cm between plants. The smaller variety is ideal for growing in a pot, which can be moved to a warm, sunny window ledge when the weather turns cool. A pot of basil standing near a doorway will help to keep those annoying summer flies away, too.

To be sure of a supply of dried basil for winter months, cut the long, leafy stalks at the end of summer, just before the plant flowers. They are best dried in the drying box described in the final chapter, as they do not dry successfully either in bunches or in a slow oven.

Basil is one of the best loved of all herbs, having a flavour that goes well with tomato, courgettes or zucchini, spinach and potato. It is one of the ingredients which makes Italian foods, such as spaghetti dishes, pizza, and bolognese sauce, so irresistible to many of us. The strongly pungent oil of basil is used in making perfumes and medicine.

BAY TREE 

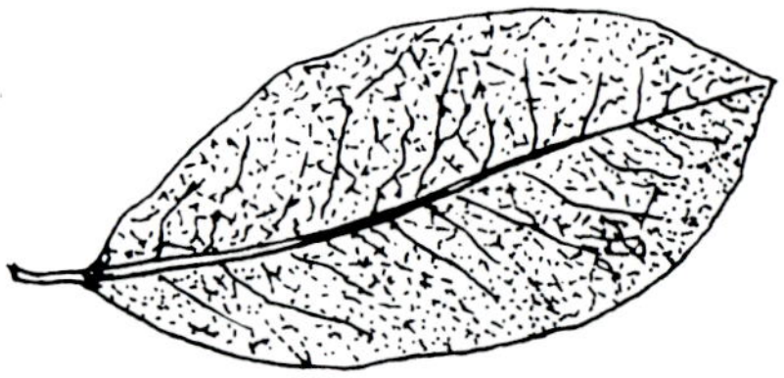

This glossy-leaved tree will grow to 12 m. However, it grows very slowly and can be planted successfully in a large pot or tub. Its full name is "bay laurel", or "*Laurus nobilis*", which indicates its ties with noble deeds and achievements. When the ancient Roman, Ben Hur, won his famous chariot race, he was crowned with a wreath of bay laurel leaves. The laurel wreath was also a token of high honour when presented to warriors and scholars. The bay has been used in healing, too, both as an oil to rub on sprains and bruises and as a tea to reduce fevers. In modern times, bay leaves are important as an ingredient of pot pourri (a deliciously perfumed mixture of flowers, herbs and spices), and for use in flavouring stews, soups and casseroles.

Bay trees can be grown from cuttings, taken when the new spring growth has had a month or two to harden. The cutting should be about 15 cm long, with at least two-thirds of the bottom leaves removed. The cuttings will probably take all summer to grow roots — be sure to keep them well watered during this time. As these plants grow very slowly, it is a good idea to keep them in pots for at least a year before planting in the garden.

The leaves can be used fresh, straight from the tree, or they can be dried. A bunch of leafy branches can be tied together and hung in a dark, airy place until the leaves are crisp, or the leaves can be taken from the branches and dried in a drying box (see Chapter 5). Once they are crisp-dry, the leaves should be stored in an air-tight container.

Have you ever seen the words *"bouquet garni"* in a recipe? This means simply "bunch of herbs" and consists of a bay leaf and a spray each of thyme, marjoram and parsley tied together. The herbs are added to a stew or casserole and cooked gently, for several hours. At the end of the cooking time the leaves will have softened and fallen into the food, and the woody stems are removed before the meal is served.

CHERVIL 

This pretty, fern-like herb was once included in all herb gardens, yet it's seldom used in the kitchen now. Its fine slender stems grow up to 30 cm tall, with soft green leaves which turn a pinkish-red in the sunlight. For this reason it is best grown in a fairly shady place and, because of its size, it can be grown easily in a pot.

Long ago, chervil was used not only in food but also in medicine. It has been taken for kidney complaints and rheumatic pains and used externally on bruises. This herb has also long been associated with Easter festivals in Europe, perhaps because it has a similar perfume to myrrh which was one of the offerings to the baby Jesus. Chervil soup is traditionally served on the Thursday before Easter.

Chervil grows from seeds, preferring a partly shaded position. As it doesn't thrive if transplanted, it is best to plant the seeds directly into the garden or pot, thinning the plants out to 9 cm apart as they grow. It is sensitive to frosts so is best planted in a sheltered spot. Although we call it an annual it can, in fact, be planted twice a year, in spring and again in autumn.

When picking chervil, take the outside leaves first so that new growth can come from the middle. These tender leaves dry best in a drying box (see Chapter 5) — oven drying is not successful.

You may have heard of *"fines herbes"* which is a delicately flavoured mixture of chervil, chives, parsley and tarragon. This blend is used in sauces, omelettes, herb sandwiches, salads and cheeses. The lacy leaves of chervil also make a pretty decoration around a group of sandwiches, hard-boiled eggs, or salad. The flavour is so delicate that the leaves should not be cooked for a long time but added only for the last few minutes of cooking.

CHIVES 

There are two kinds of chives: one with an onion flavour and a rarer one known as garlic chives. They are both quite small plants, looking rather like tufts of grass, and are easily grown in either a pot or garden. Onion chives grow about 30 cm tall and have a round blade which looks like a drinking straw if you cut it at both ends! Garlic chives are taller, growing to 60 cm, and have a flat leaf like a blade of grass. Both have splendid star-burst flowers, the onion chive flower being a bluey-mauve and the garlic chive flower white. However, you must choose between these lovely flowers and your chives, for after blooming in summer the plants will die. If the flower buds are cut off as soon as they begin, the chive plants will last for many years.

Chives are the baby of the onion family (it is said that garlic is the grandfather!). The more you pick the chives, the more energetically the plant will grow. After a year or two it may be necessary to dig up the plant and gently separate the clump into two or three parts for replanting. This is called root division and is the easiest way to increase your chives. They also grow easily from seed in a seed box and can be planted both in spring and autumn, if your winters are mild. When the seedlings are about 10 cm high, they can be transplanted to the garden or a pot. Put about ten roots in together to form a clump. If in the garden the clumps should be about 30 cm apart.

When picking chives, pinch them off with your thumb and finger. Using scissors makes the edge die back slightly and turn an unhappy-looking brown. There is no successful way to dry chives at home — the green chives that can be bought in bottles are dried by a very expensive and scientific method called "freeze drying". However, we can grow them fresh for all-year use by having a pot of them kept somewhere warm and sheltered during the cold months. Although chives are perennial (not needing replanting every year), they do tend to die back a little during winter and shoot again in spring.

Chives are a very useful herb. Their mild onion flavour can be used in almost any cooking, especially with eggs, as in scrambled eggs and omelettes. The texture of the chive leaf is so delicate that it will lose its colour and flavour if cooked for too long, so only add the chopped green leaves during the last five minutes of cooking time. Chopped chives are very attractive if sprinkled at the last minute onto chilled soups, mashed potatoes, sliced tomatoes and salads.

CRESS

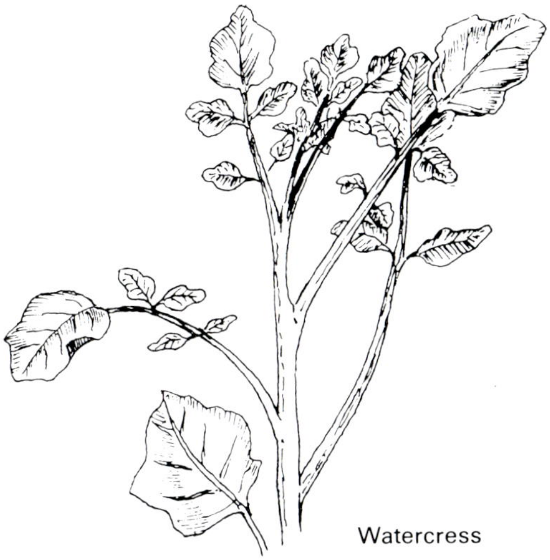

Watercress

Watercress has been a favourite salad and sandwich herb for centuries in England and Europe. It has an interesting peppery flavour, adding zing when blended with the milder herbs. Watercress is a perennial herb, growing in streams and creeks or in a very damp part of the garden. It has a creeping habit and grows only about 30 cm tall. The dark green glossy leaves are full of natural iron and vitamins, which makes it very good for keeping our blood clean and healthy. Long ago, herbalists used it to cure headaches and magicians sang of it in a chant to keep evil spirits away!

This herb can be grown from seeds started in a seed box. When the plants are big enough they can be put into the garden in a very moist, shady place. If you have a fish pond, you could try planting the watercress around the edges. The important thing to remember is that the water must not become stale; but if you have fish in it, no doubt you are already keeping the water fresh for them.

The more watercress is picked, the thicker it will grow. Constant picking during summer will stop the tiny white flowers from appearing, and all the leaves you pick can be added to salads, nibbled as a refreshing snack, or used to make delicious watercress soup.

Land Cress

Land cress comes in two or three varieties: the main ones are curled cress, which has pretty, lacy leaves something like parsley, and American upland cress, with long leaves like those of a dandelion. The flavours of these types are very similar to the hot taste of watercress. The seeds of land cress can be planted straight into the garden, with a thin layer of soil patted on top of them. They will grow quite quickly in a shady position and soon be ready for picking. Land cresses are annual herbs, but if you have winters without frosts they can also be grown all through the year.

Cress is often mixed with young mustard leaves as a sandwich filling and you have possibly seen packages for sale of cress and mustard seeds for sprouting (see page 25). The sprouts can be cut and used in about a week from sowing, which is a quick, fun way for all the family to enjoy this herb.

DILL 

This is the first of the herbs we have mentioned which gives us food not only from its feathery leaves but also from its seeds. It is a pretty, delicate herb growing to 90 cm tall. Pale yellow flowers bloom late in summer, with delicious seeds nestled inside their umbrella shape. As the stems are quite thin and soft, dill likes to be sheltered from the wind but still open to plenty of sun — against a wall or fence is a good place, or even in the shelter of a taller, stronger herb like rosemary or oregano.

Dill first came from the area around the Mediterranean, although it was well known in many parts of the ancient world. The name "dill" comes from the Norse *"dilla"* meaning "to lull", which shows us that it was used as a soothing herb. Dill water is still sometimes given to babies to prevent wind pains, and dill seeds are often cooked with foods which might otherwise give us stomach aches. Also, in times gone by, dill was one of the herbs supposed to ward off evil spells and witchcraft. When dill is used in medicines, the seeds are used in preference to the leaves, as they are much richer in the oils that have the helpful qualities. The taste of the leaves is much milder than the seeds.

Although an annual, dill can be planted twice a year, in spring and autumn, to give an all-year crop. Like chervil, it doesn't like to be transplanted

so the seeds should be planted straight into the garden or pot where the plants are to grow. Remember to keep the bed well watered, especially before the baby plants show their first green tips.

To dry the leaves, frond-like sprays should be picked before the flowers bloom (for the best flavour) and spread out in a drying box (see page 35). This is the only successful way of drying these delicate, aniseed-flavoured leaves. The seeds can be collected by cutting the flowers late in summer and spreading them on a tray or sheet of newspaper in the sun for a few days. By then they should be completely dry and the seeds will shake out easily onto the tray. You can then put the seeds into an air-tight bottle, where they will keep for years.

Dill is usually combined with two particular foods — fish and the salad vegetable that goes so well with fish, cucumber. No doubt everyone has seen dill pickles in the supermarket or in the pantry at home. Fresh dill can be chopped and sprinkled on grilled or steamed fish. It also combines well with sliced cucumber, cooked peas or potatoes.

The aromatic, spicy seeds are delicious in cooked cabbage and are an essential addition to cole-slaw (raw cabbage salad), chutneys and pickles. We have a friend who tosses cooked courgettes or zucchini in butter and dill seeds before serving, and the result is mouth-watering!

2

GERANIUMS

The most sweet-smelling and easily grown plants in a herb garden are the various scented members of the geranium family. We all know well the kind of geranium that gives us bright, colourful flowers, but it doesn't exactly have an inviting aroma! But there are many scented geraniums, including rose, lemon, peppermint and nutmeg. They are all quite hardy once established and all love plenty of sunlight, except the peppermint geranium which thrives in moist, shaded places. The peppermint geranium looks different, too, having a large, green, furry leaf and a soft, fleshy stalk. Rose and lemon varieties have leaves with a more ragged or frilly edge, while the little nutmeg geranium has leaves smaller than a baby's hand and delightful, delicate, white flowers. The peppermint also has white flowers, though small and not at all showy, and the rose and lemon types have mauve and pink flowers.

All geraniums can be easily grown from cuttings, following the instructions in Chapter 3. Once you have these plants they will be with you for years, being very strong growers. The rose, peppermint and lemon types will grow as tall as 1 m and it is a good idea to cut back some of the growth at the end of each summer just to keep these hearty plants under control. Nutmeg scented geraniums grow to about 40 cm tall and grow well in garden borders, where they will always look attractive.

Peppermint Geranium

Rose Geranium

When harvesting scented leaves, cut off whole branches using secateurs (garden clippers), then cut off each leaf separately. (The bare branch without the leaves can be used as a cutting for starting another plant.) These leaves can only be dried using the drying box method (see page 35) and will take longer than most other herbs to become crunchy-dry. You must be absolutely sure that they are dry before using them in sachets or pot pourri, or they might go mouldy and waste all your good work.

The main use for scented geraniums is in making perfumed gifts (see Chapter 5), but the lemon or peppermint leaf can also make a pretty setting for curls of butter at a lunch or tea-party, and the rose or nutmeg leaves can be used to line the bottom of a cake tin before pouring in the batter. After the cake has been cooked and turned out to cool, you simply peel the leaves off the base. The gentle flavour of the leaves will have cooked into the cake, making an ordinary sponge cake into a praise-winning delicacy. You could use this method to make mother an extra-special birthday surprise cake, topped with whipped cream.

LAVENDER 

A must for every scented garden, lavender is easy to grow and very rewarding as it blooms for most of the year. There are many different types, including a white-flowered variety, but the main ones are English, French and Italian lavender. All thrive in a sunny, well-drained position and need little care, except for cutting back fairly severely at the end of flowering. The strong aroma of lavender must surely be one of the best-loved in the world, being used not only for perfuming drawers and linen cupboards but as an addition to the bath. What a sumptuously relaxing sensation to sink into a warm, lavender bath at the end of a long day! It has a very soothing effect and prepares one delightfully for sleep. Lavender oil has always been added to childrens' baths to ensure a good night's sleep not only for them but also for their weary parents!

Italian lavender: This one always seems the "baby brother" being only 60 cm tall, and has a darker but much smaller flower than the others. Branches of the smooth, grey leaves were used long ago as "strewing herbs" to cover the floors of Spanish homes and churches. Imagine the sweetness of the air after many passing feet have bruised the lavender and released that lovely perfume. When your lavender bushes have grown big, you might like to use them as strewing herbs — but not on a carpeted floor, and only if you are prepared to clean up after you!

French lavender: The hardiest of the lavender family, it can grow as tall as 1.5 m, even after being cut down to about 30 cm every year just before spring. This pruning makes plenty of healthy new growth for the following year. French lavender has the added advantage of having the pungent oil in its dark, serrated leaves as well as in the flowers. This means that the leaves can also be used for filling sachets, giving much more quantity from each bush.

2

English lavender: In spite of its name, this, like all lavender, is native to Mediterranean regions and was not grown in England until nearly 1600. This variety grows to a height of 90 cm and has long, smooth, grey-green leaves. The tiny purple flowers appear at the end of very long, bare stems and have perhaps the strongest perfume of all the lavenders. For this reason, this is the type most often used for the making of lavender oil and filling for gifts and pot pourris.

Lavender will grow from either seeds or cuttings and, being perennial, does not need to be replanted each year. Seeds should be planted in seed boxes in spring or autumn, following the instructions in Chapter 3. Take cuttings in late spring, when the new growth has hardened. (Cuttings of soft new growth will wilt and die.) When they are well rooted the young plants can be planted out into a sunny, well-drained position. Any of the lavenders make very attractive hedges when planted 50 cm apart beside a path or above a retaining wall. Once established, the bushes will bloom constantly for about nine months of the year. As each flower passes its best, it should be cut off at the place on the stalk where two new shoots branch at either side. This helps to keep the bush thick and well shaped, and the plant is more attractive without brown, finished flowers amongst the purple.

Harvest the lavender at any time of the year, on a dry day before the sun has become too hot. The leaves can be stripped from the branches either green or dried. Either the bunched or drying box method is good (see page 35). When thoroughly dry, the leaves and flowers can be kept in a box or air-tight container until you are ready to make pot pourri, lavender bags or sleep pillows. You will find instructions for all of these in Chapter 5. You can also mix lavender flowers with peppermint leaves to make a fragrant, delicious tea to help you sleep. It is wonderful for unwinding after a lot of study or concentration.

LEMON VERBENA

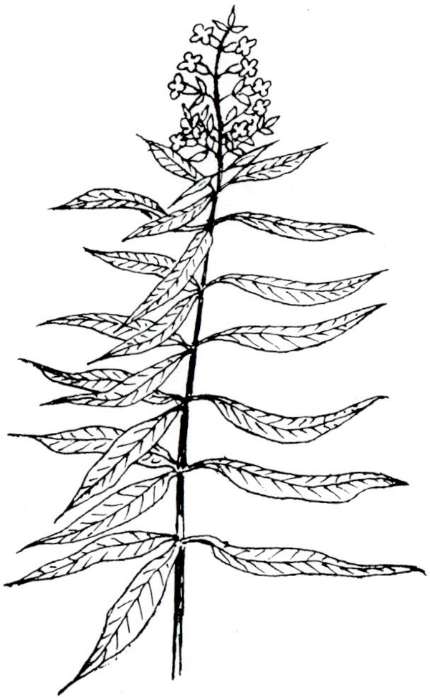

This small, deciduous tree grows to a height of 3—5 m, although it can be kept smaller by strict pruning. During the spring and summer months the tree is covered with long, pointed leaves with a strong lemon fragrance and each long, straight branch is topped by cones of airy, pale flowers. This is such a pretty tree, and it gives its citrus aroma so generously, that you should have at least one growing close to a window or verandah where you can enjoy it to the full.

Lemon verbena came originally from Chile and was not seen in European countries until it was introduced to England in 1784. It is mainly recognised for its use in making herb pillows, sachets and pot pourri. According to the Greeks, the light, fresh perfume will bring sweet dreams. I have also been told by an old Spanish lady that in her country it is used often to make a refreshing tea.

The scented leaves begin to turn yellow in autumn and by mid-winter the branches are quite bare. (Trees grown in very sheltered spots may not lose all their leaves.) This is the time to trim the branches back neatly (once the tree is three or four years old, but not before). The off-cuts can be trimmed into pencil-sized pieces and used as cuttings to start new trees. A number of sticks can be put into the one pot of sand and, if kept watered during winter, you will see small green shoots appear when spring comes. When there are roots coming out of the bottom of the pot, the cuttings can be tipped out and gently separated ready for planting.

Lemon verbena trees like a sunny position sheltered from too much wind. They also prefer a frost-free position — if this is not possible, they should be protected in winter by straw or grass clippings placed around their roots.

The leaves can be picked any time during spring and summer — once they begin to yellow, the best perfume is past. It is quite easy to strip the slightly sticky leaves off the long stems and they will dry easily in a drying box or in a gently warm oven. In the last chapter you will find instructions for making lemon verbena sachets and herb pillows.

MARJORAM AND OREGANO

These herbs are like brothers in the same family, oregano being originally a kind of wild marjoram. They are slightly different in appearance, marjoram being a smaller plant growing to 45 cm, while oregano grows to 60 cm. They are strong, hardy plants which thrive in a sunny position in well-drained soil, though they have been known to grow quite well in heavy soils, too. The same plants will grow for many years, lasting well if you cut out some of the old woody branches before each spring.

In ancient Egypt, marjoram was dedicated to the Sun god, Osiris. The Greeks also found this herb very valuable, both for dressings on bruises and sprains and for treating convulsions. It was also used as a strewing herb, that is, placed around the house to keep it smelling fresh and sweet.

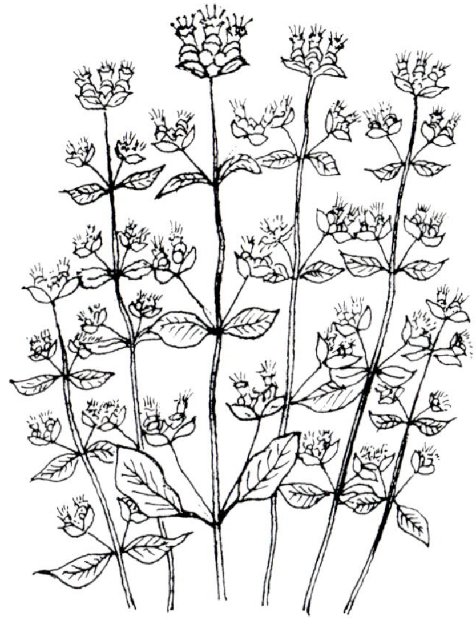

Both these herbs can be grown from seeds or cuttings. Seeds can be sown into seed boxes twice a year, in spring and autumn. They can be put out into a pot or garden bed when they are 8—10 cm tall. Cuttings can be taken in late spring or early summer, following the instructions in Chapter 3. If you are putting in more than one plant, leave at least 30 cm between each one.

Although these two herbs are very similar, marjoram's leaves are smaller and softer than its brother's. Also the marjoram grows as a neat, upright bush while oregano is a little more sprawling and untidy.

To dry the leaves, pick a bunch of long stems in late summer when the plants are bearing their tiny white flowers. Tie the stalks together and hang to dry in a dark, airy place until the leaves start to fall off. Oregano has a slightly stronger flavour and smell than marjoram, and the flavour of both is very strong when well dried and stored in screw-top jars.

Both these herbs are well loved by the Greeks and Italians, and are used in many of the traditional foods of these countries. Marjoram is also always included in mixed herb combinations for use in seasonings and stuffings.

MINT

The mint family is very large and includes applemint, peppermint, spearmint, eau-de-cologne mint and pineapple mint. The names of all these indicate the perfumes of their particular leaves. Pennyroyal is also a member of the mint family. All are delightful to grow near a verandah or pathway, where straying branches can be trodden on or squeezed to release the fragrance. The fresh, cool aroma will also help to keep flies and other summer pests away from outdoor living areas.

Mint was used by the ancient Greeks as an addition to the bath — what a refreshing idea! It was mentioned in the Bible and was known also in Egypt. Among its other uses was its ability to stop milk from curdling; not so important now when most homes have refrigerators but a valuable asset in those days. Our fondness for after-dinner mint chocolates is a direct result of mint's use for helping the digestion, and a tea made from peppermint can be taken to stop nausea and vomiting. This tea is also very rich in vitamin C so is worth drinking during winter to keep those miserable colds away.

Root divisions or cuttings are the best ways to grow mint. It grows easily in almost any position at all, sending out long, vigorous runners in all directions, and can become a nuisance if not constantly checked. For this reason, people often prefer to grow their mint in a pot, although if a bed of mint strays into the lawn, it can simply be mowed over! Pennyroyal can, in fact, be planted instead of grass to make an evergreen, delightfully fragrant lawn. It is so small that it doesn't need mowing for most of the year, except for mid-summer when spires of purple flowers rise 10—15 cm high. For this short time it is worth neglecting the lawnmower and enjoying the carpet of colour. The other types of mint grow 30—90 cm tall and should be cut down fairly low during winter to make way for new growth.

No doubt most of us have had mint sauce or mint jelly with roast lamb — this is made with spearmint, the best known of them all. The sweeter mints such as apple and eau-de-cologne make refreshing additions to fruit salads, summer drinks and sweet fritters.

PARSLEY

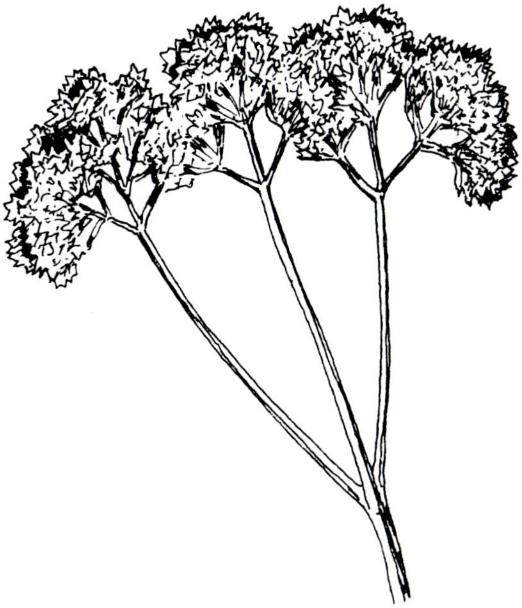

It is said that parsley goes to the devil and back three times before beginning to grow! Whether this is so or not, the seeds certainly take a long time to germinate. There are other legends linking parsley with the underworld — it was dedicated in ancient Greek myths to Persephone, who was believed to be the heart and soul of the earth. She spent half of each year in the Netherworld (underworld) and it was taken by her into the darkness of Hades. It was regarded as the key to the gate of the other side of the world. Parsley is also dedicated to Saint Peter who, it was believed, guarded the key to heaven.

The tightly crinkled, bright green leaves of curled parsley are often used to decorate grilled meats or fish so no doubt we are all familiar with its appearance and flavour. A lesser known variety is Italian parsley with leaves similar to celery tops and a faint celery flavour. This type is very useful when cooking soups and stews but is not as attractive as a garnish. It grows very easily and quickly from seed, unlike curled parsley, and grows to a height of 45 cm. The curled variety is seldom taller than 30 cm. Parsley likes a sunny, well-drained position with plenty of water.

Parsley bears flowers late in summer which are similar to, but smaller than, the dill flowers. If you want your plants to last for a year or two, these flowers must be cut off as soon as they appear. The alternative is to let the flowers come and let the plant die off — you will probably find after pulling out the old plant that a whole new crop will come up the next spring from the seeds that have fallen from the flowers.

This herb is one of the few (chervil is another) that can be dried in a warm oven, being turned over often until brittle. The bunch method is not very successful and the leaves tend to lose their bright green colour if left too long in a drying box.

Because of its lively colour and tasty flavour, parsley can be added to almost any food — salads, sauces, vegetables, casseroles, eggs or grills. When blended with chives, tarragon and chervil it forms "*fines herbes*" and it also teams with bay leaves, marjoram and thyme to make a "*bouquet garni*", both expressions which you may have seen in recipe books.

ROSEMARY 

This fresh, pine-scented herb has always been linked with remembrance. In Shakespeare's play, *Hamlet*, poor mad Ophelia collects a bouquet of flowers and herbs, saying: "There's rosemary, that's for remembrance; pray, love, remember; and there is pansies, that's for thoughts." Even in the days of ancient Greece, rosemary was believed to stimulate the memory, and Greek scholars wore garlands of it in their hair when they studied.

Rosemary is one of the tallest of the herbs used for cooking, growing up to 1.5 m. Its long, straight branches are covered with slender, spiky leaves and in autumn and winter these branches are topped with lovely, pale blue flowers. Its smaller brother, the low-growing prostrate rosemary, is often seen in rockeries and pots, and bears a lot more flowers. Both types grow best in a sunny, open position in well-drained soil.

Although it can be grown from seed, it is much easier and quicker to plant cuttings of rosemary.

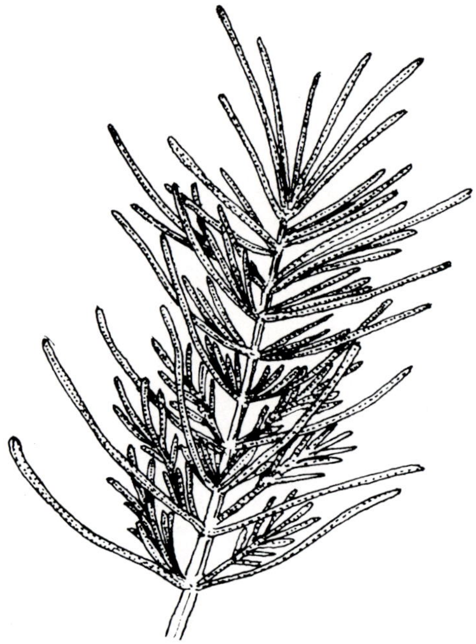

Seeds can be planted in a seed box in both spring and autumn or cuttings can be taken in late spring when the new growth has hardened. Young plants should be kept about 60 cm apart when put into the garden. The best time to harvest rosemary for drying is late summer, when the long, stiff branches can be bunched together and hung in a shady, airy place. When they are quite dry, the leaves can be stripped off and kept in an air-tight jar.

The warmly pungent flavour of rosemary goes well with foods of Mediterranean origin, including lamb casseroles, eggplant, courgettes or zucchini, and sauces for spaghetti. The leaves, both fresh and dried, are rather brittle and need to be finely chopped before they are added to cooking. When roasting a leg of lamb make two or three slashes across the meat and push a sprig of rosemary into each cut before roasting — it will make the meat delicious. Add it in moderate amounts to butter, along with dill, thyme and garlic, for herb bread.

SAGE

This hardy, 90 cm tall herb has attractive, large, silvery-grey leaves which make an appealing contrast amongst other green herbs. In autumn, the flowers turn like purple mouths to drink in the warmth of the sun. It is the sun that stimulates the plant to produce a lively, aromatic oil which gives it its strong but not unpleasant taste. It likes to grow in a sunny and well-drained place — as with most herbs, the more sunshine, the more flavour.

"Sage" is an English word meaning "wise", and the Latin name "*salvia*" is taken from the verb "*salvare*", to heal or preserve. We can see from this that sage was believed to preserve the eater, who would live to old age and wisdom. An Arabian proverb said: "How can a man die who has sage in his garden?" It was used to forestall the weaknesses of old age, as well as to help the digestion and heal sore gums and throats.

Cuttings of sage can be taken in early summer and when roots have developed they can be planted out, leaving 60 cm between each one. Seeds should be sown in spring and kept in a seed box until they are 10 cm tall. After they have been put into your garden, they should be kept well watered until the youthful green leaves turn grey. Once this change has come, they will need watering only in dry weather. (It seems to be a general rule that grey-leaved plants need less water than their green-leaved friends.) Branches can be cut for drying in late summer and dried by the bunch method (see page 35) — at the same time, any dead twigs should be cut away from the bush. The dried leaves can be kept for a long time in an air-tight container.

Sage is useful in helping us digest our food, so it can be used with rich foods such as pork, duck or goose. Those of you who have read *The Tale of Jemima Puddleduck* will remember how the fox read recipes for sage and onion stuffing for roast duck, while poor Jemima was quite innocent of his wicked intentions! This herb also makes ordinary scones and dumplings delicious, as well as being an ingredient in mixed herbs which are used in meat loaf and hamburgers.

SAVORY 

There is a perennial type of savory known as winter savory and an annual known as summer savory. Although the annual variety has a slightly stronger flavour and so is thought to be better for drying, we will deal only with winter savory which is less bother to grow. This is a rather stiff little bush growing about 30 cm tall, with thin and brittle dark green leaves. It is popular as a bordering herb hedge for formal gardens.

Savory is native to the Mediterranean countries where one can imagine it growing hardily everywhere from pebbly hillsides to fertile plains. In the Middle Ages it was used to make medicines for treating colic, giddiness and bronchitis. Used in cooking, it helps to make food more easily digested, especially members of the bean family. In many European countries it is known still as the ''bean herb''.

Winter savory seeds can be started in a seed box in spring and also in autumn in mild climates. When they are 8—10 cm tall, they can be planted out into a sunny position, 30 cm apart. If you want a hedge of savory, put the seedlings closer together, about 20 cm apart. This herb will also grow from cuttings.

Tiny white flowers bloom on winter savory in late summer and autumn. The best time to harvest the branches is just before this flowering time, and either the bunch method or the drying box can be used for drying. Store the leaves in air-tight containers once they are dry.

The leaves have a sharp, fairly hot flavour and can be used instead of pepper if you find pepper just a little too hot and spicy. The dried leaves tend to be very brittle and you may notice that they do not soften well in cooking. For this reason, they are often ground to a powder before being used. Savory may be used as an addition to hot buttered beans as well as bean salads and lentil or pea soup. Its flavour also goes well with fish, pork and veal. Savory tea is helpful for relieving chest colds and stomach aches.

THYME 

This tiny-leaved perennial is one of the best loved of all herbs. Bees love its flowers, too: the world-famous honey from Mount Hymettus, in Greece, owes its wonderful flavour and sweetness to the wild thyme growing there. The Mediterranean area is the native home of the thyme family and it is said that it grows with more flavour there than anywhere else in the world.

There are several kinds of thyme, including some that can be grown like lawns, but the most commonly used are garden thyme and lemon thyme. Both grow in a sunny, well-drained position to a height of 25—30 cm. Garden thyme has a delicious, warm, pungent taste, while lemon thyme is delicately lemon flavoured.

Both of these herbs can be grown from cuttings or root division. If you or a friend already have a bush, it can be divided into several pieces, so long as each piece has some good rootlets attached. These can then be replanted separately. Garden thyme can also be grown from its tiny black seeds planted straight into finely dug soil and later thinned out to about 15 cm apart. Remember to keep the garden well watered until the seedlings are established. Seeds for lemon thyme often produce a less aromatic plant than the original and for this reason are not easily available in shops and nurseries. These herbs bear attractive flowers in different shades of pink during spring and summer. The bushes should be cut back fairly hard after flowering, and should be replaced after a few years.

Branches for drying should be taken before the plants begin to flower, as this is when the flavour is best. They can be dried using either the bunch method or in a drying box. The crisp leaves can be stripped from the branches and kept in an air-tight jar.

The oil from thyme, thymol, is a strong antiseptic and is included in cough drops. Fresh or dried thyme is used to season stuffings for meat, fish and poultry, or on its own as an addition to hamburgers and paté. The fresh, light taste of lemon thyme is an appealing addition to fish and chicken and makes a deliciously refreshing summertime tea.

Getting started

Growing herbs from seeds

A simple, dry seed can be brought to life by giving it water. It is easy to imagine the first small roots beginning to grow and the tiny new shoot pushing its way upwards towards the light, even though, of course, we can't see under the soil. It often takes about a week from planting a seed to seeing the shoot come out of the ground and that week is very important indeed. Once the seed has been given that first water to bring it to life, we must be sure that it is always moist. Just one day without water is long enough for it to die of thirst and no amount of watering later will revive it. However, it is also important not to make the soil around the seed too wet or the seed will turn sour and die. The best test is to feel the top of the soil with your finger — if the very top grains or soil are turning dry and sandy, it is time to water again.

Using a seed box

Most herbs are best started in a seed box in a warm, sheltered, shady place. The lid of an egg carton makes an effective and cheap seedling tray, and you can make a hot-house effect by spreading a piece of plastic over the top. This helps to keep the seed warm and moist, which makes it grow more quickly.

Fill your seed tray with either a commercially packed potting mixture (available from a plant nursery or garden department of a large store) or your own mixture made from one-third sand and two-thirds light, loamy soil. Add a little peat moss if you can, as this helps to hold the moisture. (You can also buy peat moss at nurseries.) Never use sand from the seaside for growing seeds, as it contains salt. Pat the soil down well with the palm of your hand before planting the seeds. Sprinkle the seeds lightly in rows on top of the soil. Then, using an extra handful of potting mixture, sift a thin covering over the top of the seeds. Once again, pat it all down firmly with your hand, then water well using a gentle spray. (A strong spray of water might uncover or move the seeds.) Spread a piece of plastic over the top of the tray. Water the seed tray at least once a day until the shoots show above the soil.

The baby plants, or seedlings, can be left in the seed tray until they are about 8 cm tall. In the meantime, you can remove any of the seedlings which look thin and weak, leaving only the strongest to be removed to your herb pot or garden. If the plants are to be put into the garden, it is often a good idea to let them have an "in-between" time in a pot about 10—15 cm deep,

1

4

during which time the root system will grow strong and healthy. The pot should be kept in a place where your plant can receive a little sunshine in order to prepare it for its later sunny position.

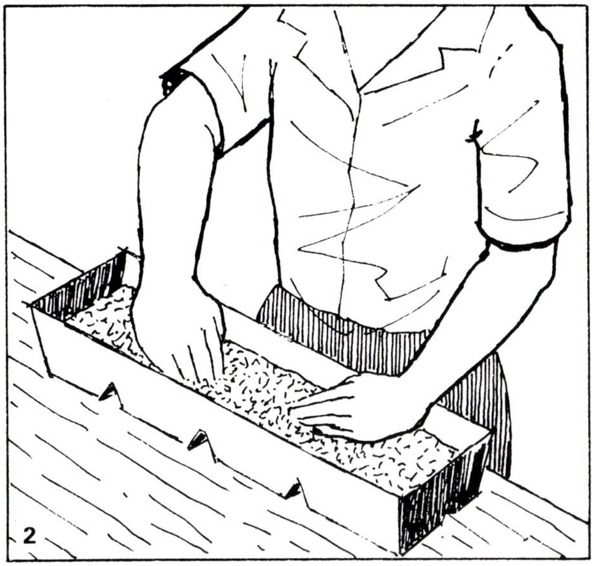

2

3

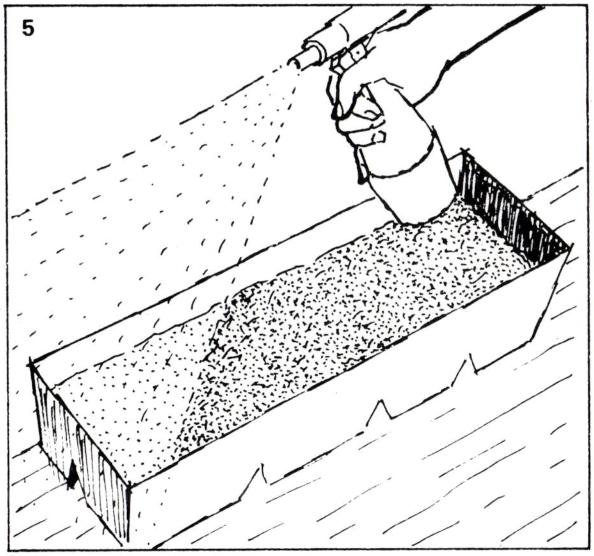

5

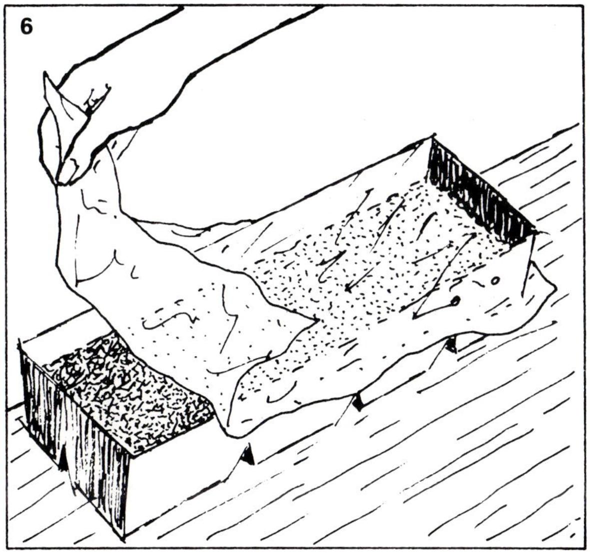

6

Growing herbs from cuttings

Taking a cutting from someone else's plant is a quicker way to have a new plant than planting a seed, but not all herbs will grow successfully from cuttings. (See the descriptions of each herb in Chapter 2.) The cutting must be taken from a strong part of the bush; if it is a young, soft part it will die before growing roots. Late spring, when the new growth has had time to firm, or autumn are the best times to take cuttings. Use scissors or secateurs (special garden clippers) to make a clean cut and carefully remove the lower leaves by pulling them *upwards* or cutting them off. Never tear the leaves downwards off a cutting.

Have ready a pot of wet river sand which has been patted down well so that it is packed firmly. Using a knitting needle, pencil or straight stick, make a hole in the sand. Then put the cutting into the hole so that only one-third of the piece is above the sand. You can put several cuttings into the one pot. Keep the cuttings well watered — as with the seed tray. You can also pull a plastic bag down over the cuttings to make a little hot-house to help them to grow quickly.

Leave the cuttings in the pot of sand until there are roots beginning to grow out of the drainage holes in the bottom of the pot. Pieces taken in autumn can be left in pots all winter and moved in the spring. At this stage you should have your pots and potting mixture ready so that the new plants can be moved into a pot each. Carefully tip the pot of sand up, catching it with your free hand as the sand and roots come out of the pot. Then gently shake each batch of roots free of the others until they are all separate. They can now be potted as described in the "Herbs in pots" section on page 33. The herbs can be left in pots or, after three or four weeks, planted in the garden.

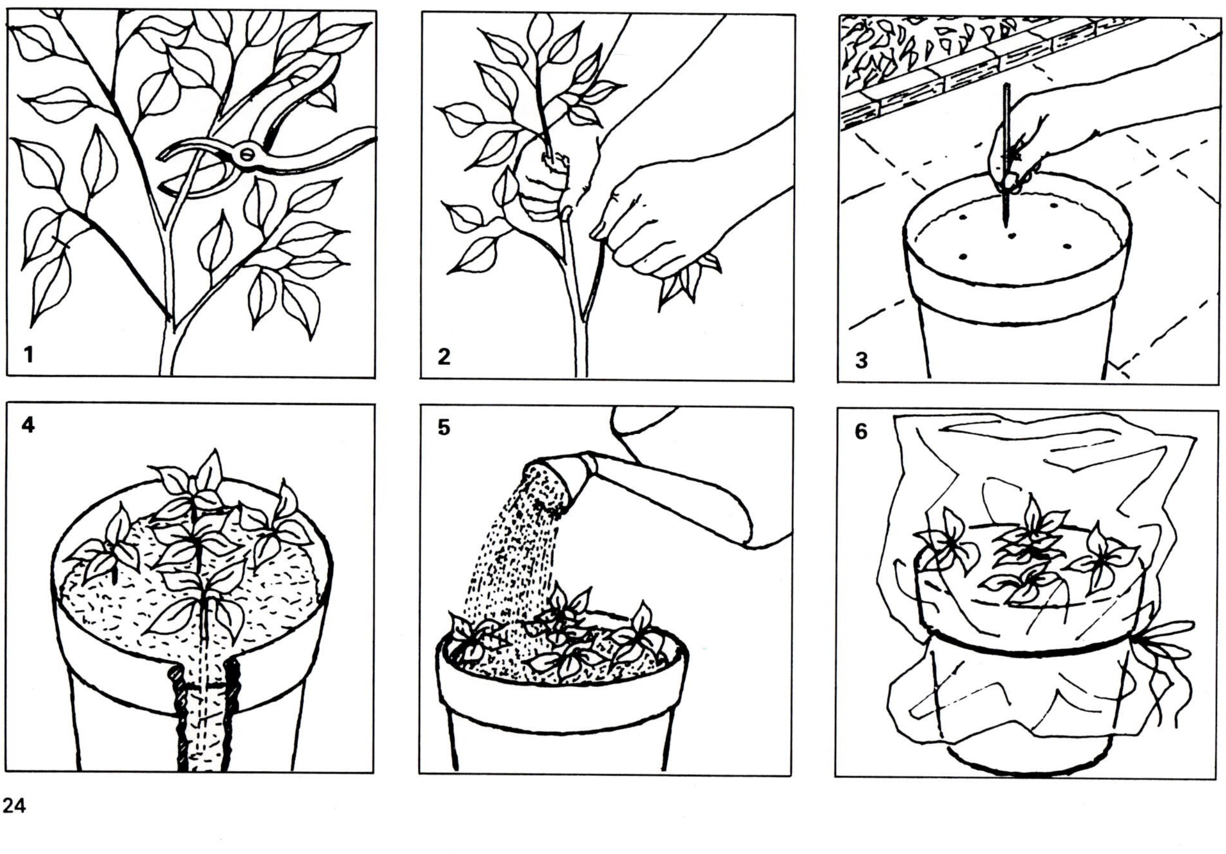

3

Sprouts

Sprouts are seeds which have been brought to life with water and allowed to grow a soft green shoot before being eaten. They are very easy to grow and fun to watch as the miracle of their new life unfolds day by day. They are ready to eat about one week after beginning. As what you eat is a complete living plant (roots and all!) sprouts are very high in food value and a worthwhile addition to your diet.

Many different seeds can be sprouted: among them are lentils, mung or Chinese beans, alfalfa, cress and mustard. The seeds can be bought at a health food shop or in seed packets from a nursery.

There are two ways of sprouting seeds, both very easy. Perhaps you have already learned about sprouting at school.

For the first method, you will need an empty jar (about the size of a medium honey or coffee jar) and a piece of thin material or a strip cut from some clean nylon stockings. Place a dessertspoon of seeds in the jar, then stretch the gauze over the top and keep in place with a rubber band. Add some water and let the seeds soak for a minute before straining all the water out again. Shake the jar to be sure all the excess water has gone, then put the jar on its side away from direct sunshine. Water it every morning and evening in the same way, and you will be able to watch your dry little seeds turn into delicious tender morsels of food. In about seven to nine days, you will see tiny leaves forming, and when the first two green leaves come is the best time to eat your sprouts.

The other way to sprout seeds is to put a layer of cotton wool or paper towel on a plate, then sprinkle the seeds on top. For younger members of your family, you could even cut the layer of cotton wool or paper into an animal shape, or maybe the initial of his or her name. If the wadding is kept moist at all times, your sprouts will grow in the same manner as for the first method.

When they are ready to use, those that you don't eat straight away can be kept in a dish of water in the refrigerator.

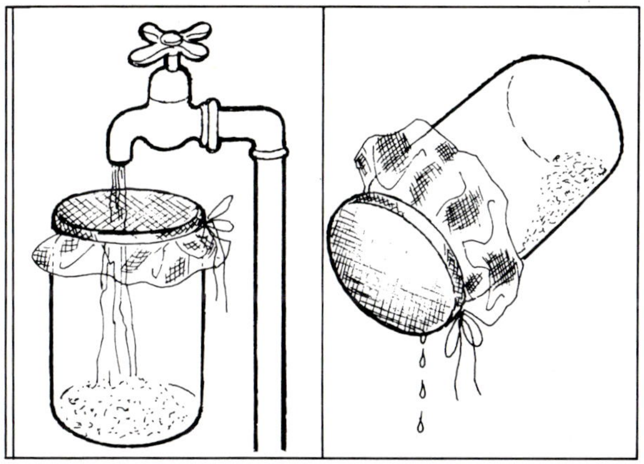

Where to plant

Rockeries

Some homes on sloping land have rockeries built into the hillside with gaps between the rocks where plants can grow. If you have a rockery, and if it gets sunshine for at least half the day, then you are lucky enough to have a perfect spot to grow some herbs. This is a good place to grow some mint, as it will be restricted by the rocks. There are several pretty and sweet-smelling kinds, such as applemint, spearmint, peppermint, and eau-de-cologne mint. The thyme family also has many different kinds — some that creep along the ground, some with silver leaves, and one with yellow leaves and a lovely lemon fragrance and taste. There is also a lemon-scented thyme with green leaves. All of these would grow well in a rockery and would spill attractively over the surrounding rocks. Other herbs to add would be prostrate rosemary, pennyroyal, and parsley.

An easy informal herb group

There are many ways of making a herb garden that can grow piece by piece as you find more that you want to grow. For instance, many homes have a letter-box or a birdhouse or birdbath standing all alone in the lawn, but it could be the focal point in a pretty, fragrant garden. Of course, you must make sure that the postman can still reach the box easily! You could start this group with maybe just a bay tree, lemon thyme and wormwood, adding the others as you go.

The herbs in the sketches are only suggestions; you can use whichever ones you like best. The annual herbs included will die during winter but will grow well and give lots of pleasure and flavour during the school summer holidays. A general rule when choosing herbs for your garden is to grow taller plants towards the back of the garden, and smaller ones at the front and along edges.

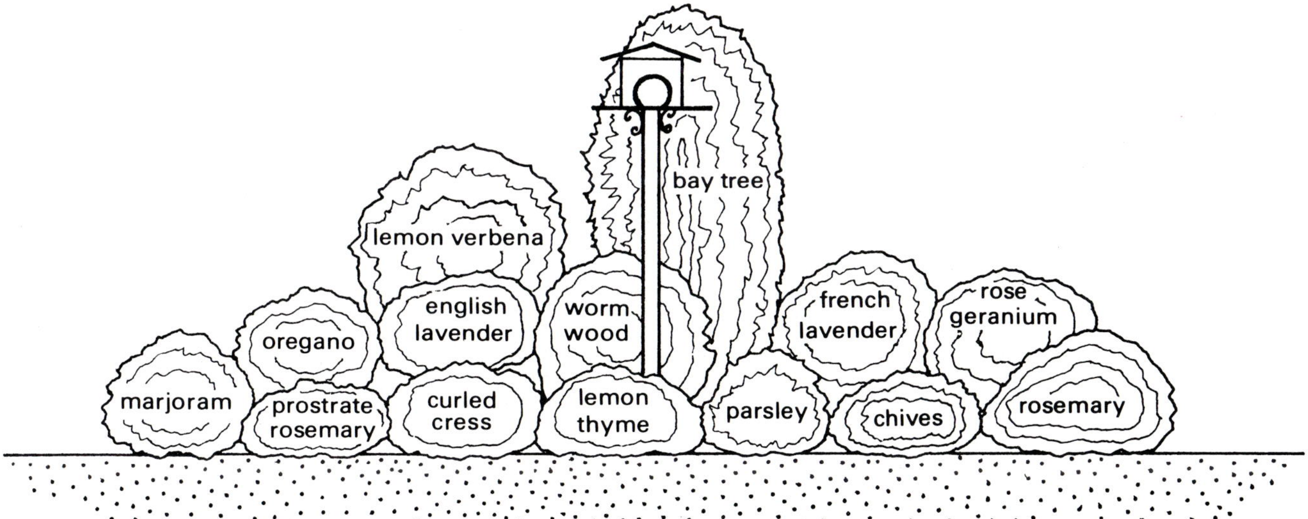

Vegetable gardens

It has been known for a long time that some herbs are good for repelling certain pests, and there are particular plants which have a good effect upon their neighbours. One of the best known of these partnerships is tomatoes and basil, which not only grow well together but are delicious when eaten together.

It is easy to grow your own sweet corn — so delicious to eat even before the cobs are cooked. When you do so, plant a row of dill on either side of the corn patch to have larger and healthier plants.

Radishes are other vegetables which are quick and easy to grow. They have a good friendship with chervil.

Lettuce likes to be grown close to the carrot patch, and carrots are better if grown with rosemary, sage or chives.

Parsley, dill and lemon balm when they are in bloom will help your garden by attracting bees and butterflies, as well as looking pretty amongst the non-flowering vegetables. It is also good to include marjoram as it seems to have a good effect on all vegetables. However, be careful to avoid planting fennel, which is not helpful to any vegetables at all.

Below is a suggested layout for a small vegetable garden. You will notice that small groups of cabbage and celery are placed where they can benefit from the dill which is planted near the sweet corn. Sage has been planted where it can help repel the white cabbage butterfly, while still close enough to the carrots to repel the troublesome carrot fly. By adding a few chive plants amongst your carrots, your carrot crop will be especially big and juicy.

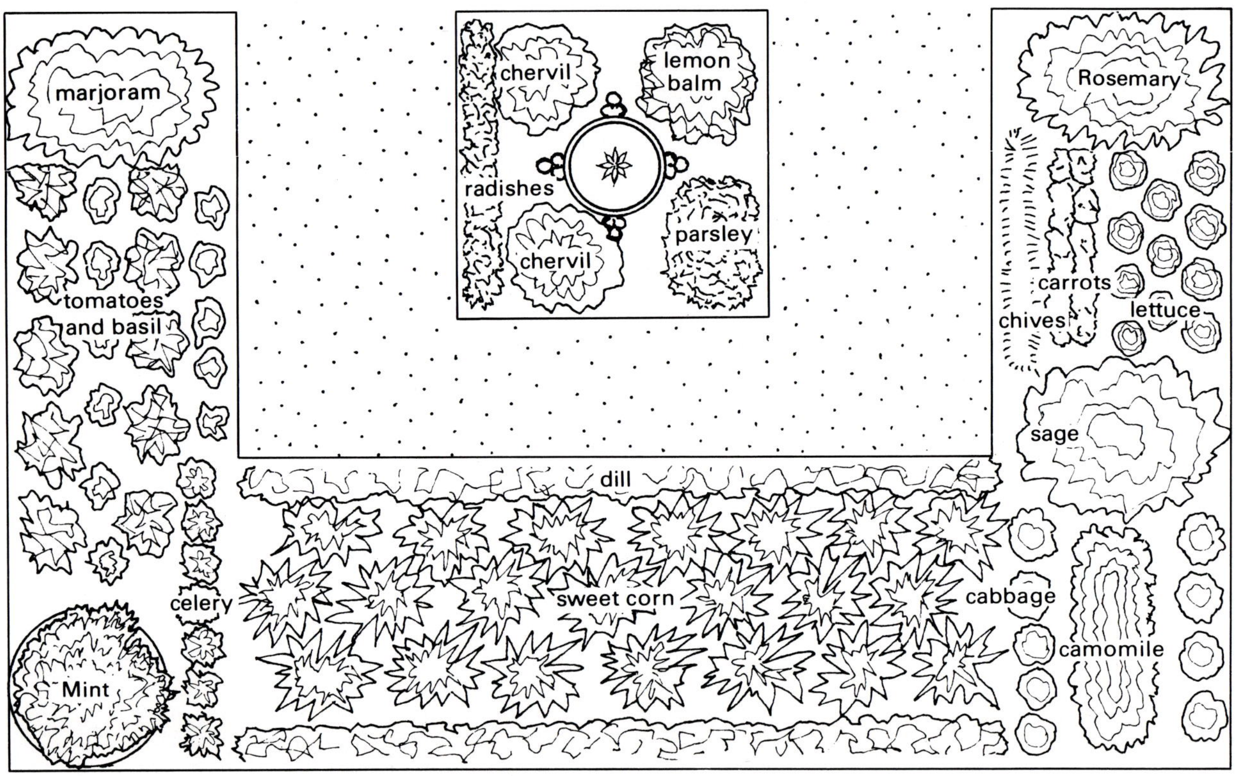

4

Herbs to repel insects

The first point that must be made about repellent herbs is that they will never have the complete and immediate effect of a can of chemical spray. However, it has been proven that the more repellent herbs used and the longer they are there, the better the effect. Placing these herbs where the leaves can be pinched or trodden on to release the aroma also helps to make them more effective.

Those of you who own a horse or pony may like to plant a walnut tree beside your horse's stable — as a long-term project! These trees repel stable flies, and your animal will like to stand under it. How delicious, too, to pick your own fresh juicy nuts straight from the tree in the summer time! Basil, tansy and rue also help to keep flies away, and can be planted in clumps near doorways.

Mint is one of the best repellent herbs as it is useful against ants, aphids, cabbage butterfly caterpillars, fleas, beetles and moths. In Chapter 6 you can find out how to make flea and moth repelling sachets.

Pennyroyal is a low-growing, strong-smelling cousin to the mint family. It is a good repellent of flies, fleas and mosquitoes. Most of the year its growth is even lower than the average lawn, except in December when it grows to about 10 cm and bears a pretty purple flower. We have planted it under the clothes line where it grows with the grass quite happily, and there is no risk of insect bites whilst hanging out the clothes! There is also the added enjoyment of pennyroyal's strong minty aroma, which is released when it is walked on. It has a creeping type of growth and is constantly spreading to cover more and more ground.

Another useful herb is wormwood, which can be used to keep moths, flies and fleas away. It is a tall, handsome herb with silvery-grey leaves and a strong, pungent smell. You could grow it in a fairly large pot somewhere close to your kitchen or laundry door to help keep the flies away. Unfortunately it has a very bitter flavour, as does rue, and neither of them can be used in cooking.

The old-fashioned herb garden

This must surely be one of the most satisfying types of garden to have, although it takes quite an amount of work and, once it's growing, you must be prepared to keep it tidy and free of weeds. Herbs like to grow in well-drained light or sandy soil. If your soil is heavy and lumpy dig it well with a garden fork, at the same time adding some compost or well-dried fowl manure.

4

Your parents will probably be happy to help you prepare the ground for your garden. Remember that the better you have dug and forked over the soil, the better your garden will be.

If possible, choose a sunny, open spot for your herb garden, as this is the position that most herbs like. If one side can be bordered by a building or fence, a sheltered position will be available for those herbs needing it (see Chapter 2). Tidy paths are important so that you can reach all the herbs easily. The paths can be made from bricks, pebbles, lawn or scented low-growing herbs such as pennyroyal, creeping thyme or German camomile. These will grow thickly like a lawn and give a pleasant fragrance when they are walked on; however, if you use them on your pathways you will have to keep the edges well trimmed.

Here is a herb garden plan you might like to follow:

Herb gardens can also be planned in the shape of a whole or part cartwheel. If you are lucky enough to have an old cartwheel, you can remove every second spoke, paint the wheel white and set it into the ground. Each segment can contain a different herb, but leave out varieties such as mint, which tend to creep and take over. This style can also be made without a wheel, using bricks or strong pieces of wood to mark out the shape.

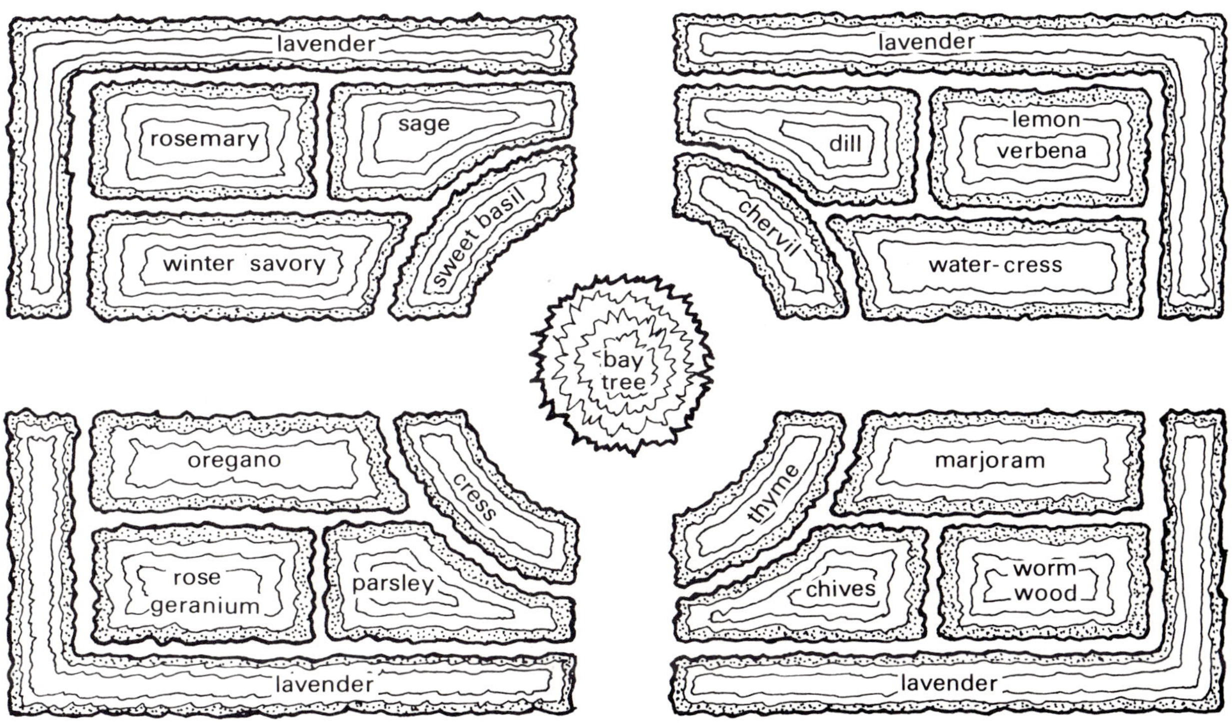

Herbs in pots

4

Even if you live in a flat or apartment with no garden space, you can still grow your own herbs. All you need is a little space on the balcony, or a place near a window where your plants will have light, sunshine and fresh air. Perhaps you have a desk or table in your bedroom that is suitable; or maybe mother will spare some of her kitchen bench for you, in return for some fresh herbs for her cooking.

You will find when you are shopping for a pot that there are lots of pretty ones to choose from; some that will hold more than just one herb, and some that hang. Remember that if you are hanging a pot when it is full of wet soil it will be quite heavy and will need a good strong hook to hang from.

There are ready-packed bags of potting mixture available from most nurseries and garden centres which are easy to use straight from the bag. You can also make your own potting mixture using two measures of river sand, four measures of light loam, and half a measure of dry cow manure. The measure can be a jam tin or a bucket, depending on how much you need.

Always place some pebbles or broken crockery in the bottom of the pot before adding the soil, so that the water will be able to drain away without letting the soil leak out the hole in the bottom! A handful of gravel from the side of the road is all you need to do the job.

Now let us suppose that you have a plant ready to put into a pot. Perhaps you have grown your own seeds or cuttings, or you might have bought the plant. Your pot should be at least 15 cm deep and the same across the top, to be sure there is enough room for the roots to grow. Place the pebbles or crockery in the bottom (enough to cover the hole properly) and cover with a handful of soil. Take your plant out of its little pot, and, holding it gently by the stem, let the roots dangle into the pot.

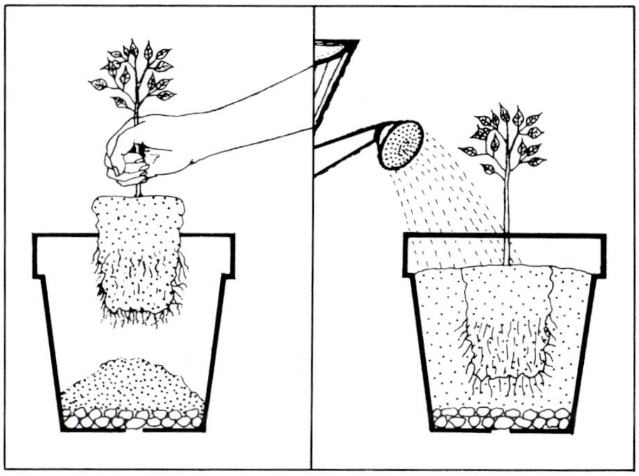

Then with your free hand, gently add more soil around the roots until they are all covered. Firm the soil down all around, and add more if necessary to bring it to the level where the roots end and the stem begins. Now your new pot plant is sitting pretty, just waiting for a drink of water and a nice sunny home.

You can use a window box or long narrow planter to make a small herb garden. Choose from any of the herbs listed, but it is best to keep any kind of mint in a pot by itself, otherwise it will wander too much and overrun everything else.

Another attractive way to pot herbs is in a strawberry pot made of baked clay which is called terracotta. It has little "pockets" around the sides where you can grow small herbs, as well as the normal top space. It is a good idea to use the top for a larger plant like sage, rosemary or sweet basil, or even a bay tree, and choose smaller ones for the pockets. Chives, thyme, parsley, marjoram, chervil, prostrate rosemary, and lemon thyme all look pretty as they spill down out of the pockets. Always plant the herbs from *inside* the pot as you are filling it with soil, rather than filling the pot right up and then trying to dig a hole through the pocket.

The best herbs to choose from when you are planning a pot are:

	Height
Sweet basil	75 cm
Bush basil	30 cm
Chervil	30 cm
Chives	30 cm
Dill	90 cm
Marjoram	45 cm
Oregano	60 cm
Spearmint	60 cm
Parsley	25 cm
Rosemary	1 m
Prostrate rosemary	30 cm
Sage	90 cm
Thyme	25 cm
Lemon thyme	25 cm

All of these need plenty of fresh air and sunshine, and water every day or two. In very hot weather be careful to water in the morning and evening, as water on the leaves in the hot sunshine will make them go brown, and the plant might even die.

Feeding

When herbs are growing in a garden bed, they are able to draw most of the nourishment they need from the soil around them, but when they are in a pot this is not possible. So we must "feed" the herb plants to keep them healthy. There are many different plant foods available from garden shops which have been scientifically made up to give the plant just what it needs. Some kinds are added to water and some are tablets to be put into the soil. Be careful that you use these only as often as the directions on the packet advise — perhaps an older member of the family could help you. Plants in pots need more water than those in a garden,

especially in hot or windy weather. But do not water the pot if the top part of the soil is still wet from the previous watering.

Pots on balconies should be turned around every few days, so that each plant has a period of facing the sun. If you fail to do this for a week or two, you will notice how the plant closest to the wall is leaning outwards, trying to reach the light and sunshine which it needs to keep growing. This rule is especially important if you have a strawberry pot planted with herbs.

How to use herbs

5

Drying

To use most herbs other than in cooking, it is necessary to dry them after picking. This must always be done *away from sunlight*, or the leaves will lose their aroma and colour. It is very easy to make a drying box out of a wooden fruit box and fly screening mesh or mosquito net. With a hammer, remove all of the bottom slats. Then spread a piece of mesh over the bottom, overlapping the sides, and secure with drawing pins. Set the box on bricks to allow the air to flow easily around and under it. In this drying box any herbs can dry well.

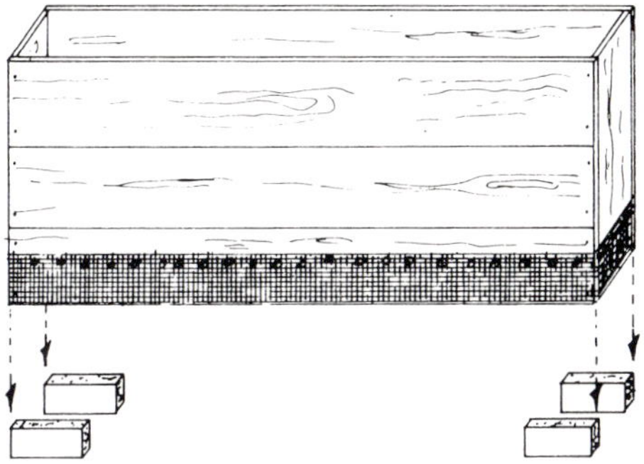

If you're in a hurry to dry the leaves, or if the weather is wet, the herbs can be spread on an oven tray and placed in an oven which has been warmed and then turned off. Never use a hot oven. Check in Chapter 2 to find out which herbs can be dried this way. Another method of hastening drying is to place your drying box in a cabinet-style clothes drier, if you have access to one. (Always check with an adult before you use a stove or dryer.)

Culinary herbs (herbs used for cooking) can be used fresh or dried. They are stronger when dried and for this process are usually picked from the base of the stems and bunched together. The stems are tied together, then the bunch is hung in an airy, dry place away from the sun. You can take a paper bag larger than the bunch of herbs and make several holes in it, slipping it over the bunch and tying it at the top. The bag allows the air to move around the leaves while still keeping the light out, and as the leaves dry and fall off, they are saved in the bag.

Things to make and do

Have you ever wondered how your pocket money is going to stretch enough to buy all your Christmas and birthday gifts? It's a problem which tends to worry everyone so here are some ideas for things to make from herbs for yourself and other members of the family and which also make great presents for friends and relatives of all ages.

Bouquet garni

If you have a relative or friend who is going to be married or is moving to a new home, this is something to delight him or her. *"Bouquet garni"* means simply "bunch of herbs" and is a mixture of parsley, bay leaves, marjoram and thyme. You can collect these from your herb garden and dry them either by the bunch method or in a drying box. When they are quite crisp, remove all the leaves from the stems and mix together in a bowl, crushing them gently with your hands to break up the bay leaves.

The material used for holding the mixture can be either plain cheesecloth or calico, or an attractive, boilproof, coloured gingham. Cut the material with pinking scissors in a circle 15 cm across — you could trace the circle first using a dish or saucer of the right size. With a needle and cotton, make a row or running stitches 2 or 3 cm from the outer edge of the circle, but instead of ending off the row, leave the thread and needle hanging.

Place a big teaspoonful of the *bouquet garni* in the middle of the material, then carefully pull in the gathering stitches all around until the filled part is a firm little ball. Tie the ends of cotton together and cut off the long ends. Now cut a 50 cm length of string and tie it tightly around the top of the ball, using a double knot to make it secure. Leave long ends of string so that the ball of *bouquet garni* can be dropped into a stew or casserole while it is cooking. The strings hang outside the saucepan lid for easy removal at the end of the cooking time. Make six of these balls and tie them together for a delightful and unusual gift.

Herbal hair rinses

A herbal hair rinse is the nicest possible way to add shine and fragrance to your hair, and is very easy to make. A rinse made with rosemary sprigs will enliven and shine dark hair, while camomile flowers will make a lightening rinse for fair hair.

Pick a bunch (about eight sprays) of whichever herb you want to use. Put the herbs in a saucepan and add three cups of water, bring to the boil and simmer gently for fifteen minutes. When it has cooled, strain the liquid and put into any attractively shaped bottles you have collected. Glass shampoo bottles or sauce bottles can be used. Label it neatly and top with a secure screw-top or cork. This will keep fresh for about three months. Use about a cupful for each rinse.

Pot pourri

A "pot pourri" is a sweet-smelling mixture of herbs, flowers, spices and oils which is usually put into a pretty jar or bowl. You can collect attractive jars during the year to fill with pot pourri at Christmas time.

Collect all, or as many as you can, of the following: rose petals, lavender, scented geraniums, lemon verbena, jasmine and orange blossom. Add a little rosemary, too, to add liveliness to the sweet collection. Dry all the leaves and flowers in a drying box or on sheets of paper. When crisp-dry, measure the flowers and leaves (large leaves should be crunched in your hands into smaller pieces) into a large container with a lid. To four cups of dried material you will need about one tablespoon of oris root powder (available from some chemist shops) or a good quality talcum powder. With this powder mix one teaspoon of ground cinnamon and one teaspoon each of one or two essential oils, for example, lavender or jasmine and lemon or pine. Add this crumbly mixture to the dried leaves and flowers, mix well, and cover. It should be left for two or three weeks and stirred occasionally. After this time, it will be ready to put into the bowls that you have collected. Pieces of cinnamon bark, whole cloves, bay leaves and dried strips of orange or lemon peel may also go into a pot pourri mixture.

You will find by experimenting that you can make a pot pourri sweeter or sharper by having more or less of the spicy ingredients, or by using different essential oils. This will depend, of course, on what is available in your area.

Lavender bags

Any of the three drying methods described can be used for drying lavender. French lavender is the best type to use, as its lovely strong fragrance is in both the leaves and flowers, while English lavender has perfume only in the flowers. You can make pretty sachets from small scraps of material (ask mother if she has any left-over pieces), and you can use any of the pretty stitches you may have learned at school.

Cut two identical shapes with pinking shears, leaving a zig-zag edge. The shape can be a heart, circle, square, or whatever takes your fancy. Stitch most of the way around the shape, just leaving a small opening for filling. Add the dry lavender , then pin the last little opening together and finish the stitching.

Bag type sachets can be made out of rectangles of material, either about 10 cm by 25 cm, or 18 cm by 12 cm. Cut the edges with pinking shears so that they won't fray then pin the two pieces together, right sides facing each other. Then sew about 2 cm in from the edges along three sides (use

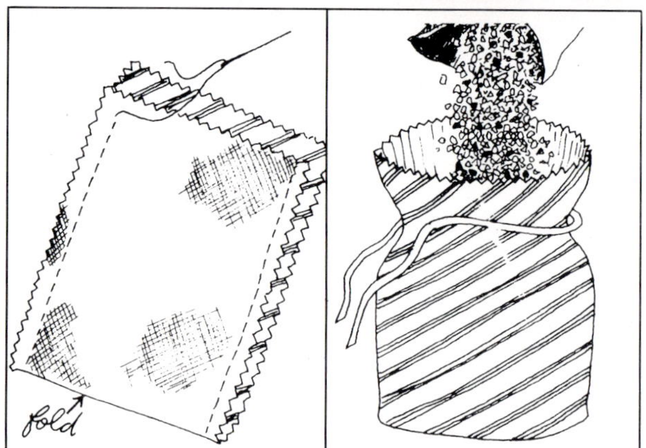

backstitch or your mother may allow you to use her sewing machine). Turn the bag to the right side and fill with dried lavender. Pull the opening together by tying with a pretty satin or velvet ribbon and you may also like to edge the top with lace.

Lemon verbena sachets

These can be made in exactly the same way as lavender bags (see page 38). It is best to pick the lemon verbena in early summer, when the fragrance is especially fresh and lemony. Strip the leaves downwards off the stem as soon as it is picked, and dry them using the drying box described or in a warm oven. The leaves will dry in about two days in normal summer weather.

Lemon verbena, like lavender, is a useful herb for keeping moths away. A sachet in each of your drawers will keep all your clothes not only moth-free but sweet-smelling and fresh too.

Herb pillows

Do you know someone who would love a sweet pillow for their bed? Herb pillows can be made in any size you like. They can be slipped in between the pillow and pillowcase, so they don't fall under the bed or get lost in the sheets.

First cut two identical shapes, any size that you want. The top side can be trimmed with lace, ric-rac or braid before the two halves are sewn together. With the right sides facing together, sew nearly all around, leaving a hole to insert the filling. Turn right sides out, fill, and stitch by hand to close the hole. Make the filling a mixture of lavender, lemon verbena, rose petals and scented geraniums. These herbs are chosen for their soothing qualities as well as their sweet perfumes. Here's how to make the filling:

To dry roses, the flower must be picked when it is just past its best blooming time, when the petals will drop easily from the hip or centre. Spread the petals out onto a sheet of paper or in a drying box and they will dry in two or three days. Gently turn or mix the petals a few times during the drying period to circulate the air. Although the dry petals will be much smaller than the fresh, they will keep their perfume and colour if you have kept them away from too much light. They are too fragile to dry in an oven.

Lemon, rose or peppermint scented geraniums can be used in herb pillows — use whichever you have growing, or a blend of all of them. You will need scissors or garden clippers to cut their thick stems. Cut them branch by branch, then remove each leaf one by one into the drying box. These fleshy leaves will take longer to dry, being thicker, and should be ready for use in about a week from picking.

Having dried all the ingredients, you can now mix them together in a bowl. Use equal amounts of lavender, each scented geranium, and rose petals, and about twice as much lemon verbena. This mixture of scented herbs and flowers will still smell sweet after a couple of years, and you will find a herb pillow a very popular gift.

Pet bags

Most pets are so much a part of the family that it doesn't seem fair to forget them on Christmas Day when everyone else has a parcel on the tree. You can make your cat or dog a bag filled with flea and fly repellent herbs to wear on its collar, and a pillow, too, to keep its basket fresh and clean. The repellent herbs to use in these bags are tansy, mint, pennyroyal, wormwood and rue. You can use all these or just a mixture of the ones you have growing.

Your pet won't mind what colour or shape its pet bag is. Any piece of left-over material will do, and you can make a small bag as described for lavender bags or a ball like the *bouquet garni* ball. Tie or sew a length of string or cord to the bag so that it can be tied to your pet's collar.

Clove orange

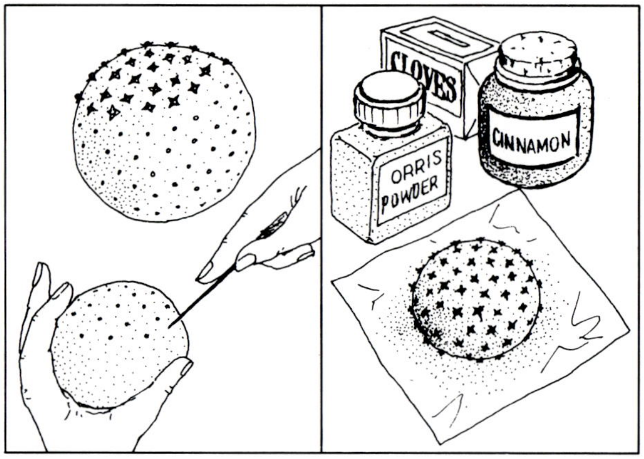

This doesn't use any of the plants from your herb garden but is worth mentioning as an attractive and easy gift. It should be made at least eight weeks before you want to give it away, so that it has time to dry and mature.

Use the freshest possible orange (or lemon or apple), picking it straight from the tree if you can. Stud it all over with cloves, leaving enough space between each clove to allow for slight shrinkage of the fruit as it dries. When you have completely covered the orange, roll it in a mixture of half cinnamon and half oris root powder (available from some chemist shops) to absorb all the stickiness. Oris root powder is made from the root of the Florentine iris — if you have trouble finding it, you can use a good quality talcum powder instead.

Now wrap your clove orange in tissue paper and put it somewhere cool and dark (a drawer or cupboard is good) for six to eight weeks, to dry out. You will need 1.5 m of thin velvet ribbon to finish off the gift. Place the middle of the ribbon on the top of the fruit using a pin to hold it there, then pull the ribbon down the sides and tie a firm knot at the base. Turn the ribbon at right angles and bring it back up to the top to another knot (you can remove the pin now). Trim the long ends of ribbon to the same length and join them with a double knot and the neatest bow you can tie. You will now have the prettiest and biggest moth ball in the street!

Cloves have strong germ-fighting properties and, many years ago, clove oranges were carried or worn to protect the wearer from diseases. They are also used to protect linen and clothing from moths as well as being attractive simply as a decoration. If you have a toothache, you can bite a clove releasing the pungent oil which will numb the pain.

Cooking

Herbs are delightful additions to our gardens, with their delicate perfumes and attractive shapes and flowers, but they will always be most valued for the exciting flavours and aromas which they add to food. Here are some simple recipes you can make yourself to try out the flavours of some of the herbs that you have grown. (Remember, always make sure there is an adult around to help you before using a stove or barbecue.)

An important point to remember when using herbs in cooking is that dried herbs are much stronger in flavour than fresh. If a recipe states, say, one tablespoon of a fresh herb, the dried equivalent would be about one-third of a tablespoon.

HAMBURGERS

500 grams minced hamburger steak
1 onion
salt and pepper
1 teaspoon chopped fresh marjoram or ½ teaspoon dried
1 teaspoon chopped fresh parsley or ½ teaspoon dried
oil for frying
buns
butter
tomato sauce
lettuce
tomato slices
beetroot slices

1. Peel and chop the onion finely and put in a bowl with the meat, salt, pepper and herbs. Mix well with a fork.
2. Shape the mixture into patties with your hands and put them aside on a plate.
3. Heat the oil in a pan or on a barbecue hot-plate. Add the patties and cook a few minutes on each side.
4. When cooked, place the patties between toasted, buttered buns, with tomato sauce, lettuce, tomato and beetroot.

GARLIC AND HERB BREAD

(For 6—8 people)

1 long French bread or 2 short ones
3 tablespoons soft butter
1 or 2 cloves garlic (depending on your own taste)

¼ teaspoon salt ½ teaspoon dried basil ½ teaspoon dried parsley ½ teaspoon dried marjoram a pinch dried sage	Dried herbs are easier, but if using fresh, double the quantities.

1. Mix the butter, herbs, salt and garlic together. Use a garlic crusher if you have one, otherwise chop the cloves as finely as you can.
2. Slice the bread to the thickness you prefer, cutting it right through at the bottom. (Have you ever tried to take just one slice of bread from a loaf of garlic bread that is still joined at the bottom edge? It's a major operation that is best avoided.)
3. Spread the butter on each slice, remaking the loaf in a baking dish as you add each slice. Fit the slices in tightly from one side of the baking dish to the other so that they hold each other in place.
4. Place in a 200°C (400°F) oven and cook for 20 minutes with no cover. (Cooking with foil on top steams the bread and makes it soggy.) Remove the bread to a serving basket or plate and serve immediately. The crusts should be crisp and crunchy, and the centres should be soft, warm and herby.

HERBED SPROUT SALAD

(For 4 people)

1 cup bean or alfalfa sprouts
1 cup cottage cheese
4 large sprigs parsley
1 spray chervil or 2 blades chives
4 lettuce leaves (large and unbroken)

1. Mix the sprouts and cottage cheese well together.
2. Break the parsley into small leaflets, about the size of your little finger-nail, and do the same with the chervil. If using chives, cut them into 5 mm lengths. Save one tablespoonful of parsley and stir the rest of the herbs into the cheese mixture.
3. Place a lettuce leaf on each of four plates, and spoon one quarter of the cheese mixture into the centre of each leaf.
4. Sprinkle the reserved parsley over the tops, and serve with sliced tomato, cucumber, and crisp sticks of carrot.

This sprout-cheese mixture also makes a good after-school snack, spread on bread or savoury biscuits.

ANGELO'S SPAGHETTI

(For 4 people)

2 tablespoons cooking oil (olive oil is best)
1 large onion
2 cloves garlic
½ capsicum
125 grams mushrooms
500 grams ripe tomatoes or 1 can peeled tomatoes
1 tablespoon tomato paste
½ teaspoon salt
2 teaspoons fresh chopped basil or 1 teaspoon dried
1 teaspoon fresh chopped oregano or ½ teaspoon dried
450 grams spaghetti
parmesan cheese

1. Chop the onion and garlic as finely as you can (without chopping your fingers!) and cut up the capsicum and mushrooms.
2. Heat the oil in a medium-sized heavy-based saucepan, and add the onions, garlic and capsicum. Sauté, stirring now and again, for 3 minutes, then add the mushrooms. Stir and cook for another 2 minutes.
3. Chop the tomatoes roughly and add to the onion mixture, with the tomato paste, salt and herbs. Bring it to the boil then reduce the heat so that the sauce is just barely simmering with the lid on. Taste it and add more salt and pepper if you wish.
4. Simmer for 15 minutes, after which you can remove the lid for the rest of the cooking time. Now cook the spaghetti in boiling salted water as directed on the packet. When the spaghetti is cooked, strain it through a colander and pour a cup or two of very hot water over to help remove the starch. When it is well drained, return the spaghetti to its saucepan and toss ½ tablespoon of oil through it.
5. Serve onto plates or dishes and pour the sauce over. Sprinkle the top with grated parmesan cheese.

MINT ICEBLOCKS

1 cup pure orange juice (bought or freshly squeezed)
½ cup sugar
1 cup water
10 — 12 sprays fresh mint

1. Boil sugar and water together until sugar has dissolved.
2. Wash mint, then bruise by squeezing tightly.
3. Add bruised mint to hot syrup and leave for an hour.
4. Remove mint, squeezing it tightly to remove all the juice and flavour.
5. Add minty syrup to orange juice, using a strainer to keep out any pieces of mint which may be left in the syrup.
6. Pour into ice-block trays and place in freezer section of refrigerator to freeze.

FROZEN REFRESHER

(An elegant version of mint iceblocks)

(For 6 people)

juice of 3 oranges
grated rind of 1 orange
juice of 2 lemons
1 ¼ cups sugar
2 cups water
1 large bunch fresh mint
1 egg white

1. Combine the fruit juices and orange rind and set aside.
2. Boil the sugar and water together in a fairly big saucepan until all the sugar has dissolved. Crush the mint roughly between your hands and add it to the syrup. Let it stand for an hour.
3. Strain the syrup into a bowl, squeezing the mint to extract as much as possible. Add the fruit juice to the syrup and put it in the freezer.
4. When the mixture is half frozen (icy around the edges but still wet in the middle), take it out and add the stiffly beaten egg white. Mix it in well, then return the mixture to the freezer.
5. When frozen, serve in tall sherbet glasses or bowls, garnished with fresh sprigs of mint.

This refreshing ice can be served as a dessert or as an opener for a summer party.

Index